Jami Burron
8/30/03
Ridgewood Ranch

Seabiscuit in his paddock at Ridgewood Ranch

Cattle Brand

C.S. Howard

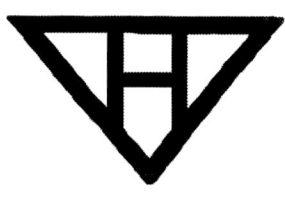

Racing Emblem

Ridgewood Ranch
Story and Photos of The 1940's

By Jani Buron

L. Buron Publishing
P.O. Box 12
Wellington, NV 89444

Copyright © Jani Buron 2002

All rights reserved. No parts of this book may be reproduced or copied in any way, shape or form, by any means without the expressed, written and dated permission of Jani Buron

First Printing May 2002

Printed in the United States of America

ISBN 0-9720755-0-X

FOREWORD

This story has always been here, in my heart, and in the hearts of those who lived at C. S. Howard's Ridgewood Ranch. With the recently renewed interest, in the year 2001, of Seabiscuit, the Howards, and Ridgewood, it is now time to finish the story I had started long ago, and share it with those readers who want to know more about those times. Ridgewood was a very special place to grow up, and we ranch kids were fortunate, indeed, to be a part of it. This is the first of what is planned to be more books on Ridgewood Ranch, in the form of a storybook, (different from a photo book), and some children's adventure books.

The name Seabiscuit brings to mind the excitement of Thoroughbred horseracing and an image of an ordinary looking little horse with extraordinary courage, speed, heart and endurance. He was a "comeback kid" kind of horse, recovering from injuries that would retire most horses from ever running again. His owner, C. S. Howard, gathered together an unlikely mix of men who attended to the horse's training and care, and they all became America's heroes as Seabiscuit went on to win some of the greatest races of all time.

When he did retire, after finally winning the famous 1940 Santa Anita Handicap, Mr. Howard brought him home to his beloved Ridgewood Ranch just south of Willits, California. A stud barn was built for the famous horse where he could retire in luxury, and his adoring fans could come and visit this racing celebrity, which they did, by the hundreds. Seabiscuit was the shining jewel in the crown of Howard's Ridgewood Ranch. However, to we children who lived on Ridgewood, Seabiscuit was just a friendly horse at the Stud Barn we used to go see now and then. Sometimes we would see Mr. Howard riding him around the ranch. We would talk to the visitors who came to see Seabiscuit and the other Howard stallions, and we wondered about all the faraway places that they came from to see this place.

That brings us to Ridgewood Ranch of the 1940's, where three happy little girls spent some of their growing-up years. This book takes the reader back to Ridgewood Ranch with photos and stories of the ranch as it was then: the Howards and their horses, the cattle roundups, the brandings, the buildings and barns, The Lake, the people of that era, and the way of life at Mr. Howard's dream ranch of self-sufficiency.

The three of us girls who lived at Ridgewood in the 1940's had such fine adventures and good times. Laverne Jones Booth and Betty Jones Peters are sisters, and they treated me, Jani (Janet) Griffith Buron like their sister, too. We rode and hiked and covered just about every corner of that 17,000 acre Ridgewood paradise. Just the three of us even rode to neighboring ranches on all day rides, with our folks permission, and with their explicit instructions on what time to be home!

Only after we moved away, the Jones family in 1949, and our family in 1950, did we realize how truly wonderful it had been to live on Ridgewood. We girls kept in touch for a lot of years after leaving and going our separate ways, but eventually our letters became fewer and fewer as we got busy raising families of our own. Pretty soon we only heard of each other now and then through mutual friends. Then, after all the publicity about the new Seabiscuit book in 2001, Laverne posted a note on a Website about living at Ridgewood, and in it she asked of my whereabouts. When I saw it, I looked up her phone number and called her immediately! We re-established contact, and she passed the word on to Betty. It had been 51 years since we had seen each other face to face, but the bond of us growing up on Ridgewood together was still there. We had a lot of catching up to do! After some long phone conversations, Laverne and I did get together face to face, and what fun that was.

I did not ever go back to Ridgewood Ranch after my family left in 1950, although my husband and I rode past the entrance gate many times on our frequent trips to Willits on business and for visits with friends and family. I was curious about how Ridgewood was after the Howards were gone, but did not want to go in and see the changes. I knew that Ridgewood, as we knew it, was gone. I wanted to remember it like it was.

Then, one unexpected morning in the final days of 2001, when we were visiting in Willits to bring in the New Year, one of my friends suggested that perhaps it was time for me to go see Ridgewood again. It had been over 51 years since I had been there. I thought about the idea for a moment, and then agreed that this may be a good time. So we drove down to the Ranch, with camera and plenty of film in hand, and started our journey down memory lane.

We met the present owners, who graciously said we were welcome to take our time and to look around freely! As we toured the ranch, and saw all the buildings and places which were so familiar, it was both emotional and gratifying. It was wonderful to see what still remained of the original place, and rather sad to see what had disappeared with the changes. We took lots of pictures. I can handle the changes now, and I know that you *can* remember a place like it *was*, as well as like it *is* ! We were invited back to Ridgewood one evening to watch the interesting movies that Doc Babcock had taken of the area many years ago.

"Seabiscuit, an American Legend" that Laura Hillenbrand so skillfully created has once again illuminated the wonderful world of Thoroughbred horse racing in that era of the 30's and 40's for younger generations to enjoy, and the older generation to reminisce in. That book touched off a myriad of my own memories, each one reminding me of the next. Ms. Hillenbrand brought back the excitement of "The Sport of Kings" to us, as well as the lesser known stories on the backstretch of all the hallelujahs and heartbreaks.

I am a student of all that. While it was expected that I follow the tradition of several other women in my family who became schoolteachers, I found that to me, my three "R's" meant Rodeo, Ranching, and Racetrack. That differed from those in the world of education who defined the three "R's" as "Reading, 'Righting and 'Rithmatic"! I did concentrate on learning, and was a good student all through school, but what always grabbed my attention were livestock and horses and riding. All that was found at Ridgewood Ranch and Willits.

The many photos in this book are identified to the best of my recollection. Undoubtedly, others who read this book will be able to identify even more of the familiar unnamed faces. That is the fun of looking at a book like this. I have identified my family members where they appear in this book using only their first names. Their full names are: my Dad, Chet Griffith, my Mom, Iny Griffith, my brother, John Griffith, and myself, Jani, or Janet Griffith Buron.

- Enjoy! -

DEDICATION PAGE

This book is fondly dedicated to:

My family and friends who were so enthused with this project upon hearing about it, and quickly encouraged me to go on with it, and offered their help and support. My sincerest thanks to each of you.

My husband, Vic, who scanned in and made the most of these small old black and white photos from my childhood picture album, and then skillfully re-worked and placed them in the proper places within the text I created. Thanks to him also for the front and back cover design, and for putting the final draft together to be printed. It all came together OK.

And lastly, this is dedicated to all those happy days at C. S. Howard's Ridgewood Ranch, way back when!

Table of Contents

a1   Title
a3   Forward
a7   Table of Contents
A   Ridgewood full page aerial map
B   Aerial map legend
a8   Tribute to Charles and Marcela Howard

2.   In the early 40's
17. In the late 40's
30. At the Willits Frontier Days
36. Ridgewood Cattle Drive and Branding
51. Ranch Kids and Horses
55. Snow at Ridgewood
56. People, Pets and Leaving Ridgewood
63. A few words about Doc Babcock
64. Epilogue
     Order blanks for gifts or friends.

A TRIBUTE TO CHARLES AND MARCELA HOWARD

Upon Seabiscuit's passing, Mr. Howard was heard to say, with great feeling :
"Seabiscuit will show them how to run up in horse heaven."

Owning Ridgewood Ranch was Mr. Howard's dream fulfilled. He bought it in the mid-20's and improved the place, building large, spacious barns and paddocks for his horses, and providing lush green pastures to feed all of his livestock. He wanted it to be a self-sufficient, productive horse and cattle ranch. He built houses for ranch families, and accommodations for the single ranch hands. It was also a place to go to for rest and country quiet, and he invited his family and friends to share it with him often.

He built a large covered reservoir above the highway to provide the ranch with plenty of good water. It is still in use today. He had an electric generator that we called "the light plant", and electricity was run to every place it was needed on the ranch. He also had a cooling room in that building where the meat was hung to age properly. There was an electrician, a carpenter, a painter, a blacksmith, and a farm machinery repairman on the ranch, and a man who drove the panel truck to town daily to deliver ranch kids to school, pick up mail, parts, and any miscellaneous items someone on the place might need.

The large dairy barn stood in the main ranch headquarters, off by itself, proudly, a little kingdom all on its own. The big healthy dairy cows were brought into the clean milking stalls at the same time twice a day. After each milking the place was judiciously scrubbed down, and the containers were washed and put out to dry. The cows were milked by hand for many years, and then Mr. Howard ordered modern milking machines brought in. Oh, the grousing and grumbling we heard from the milkers for awhile, until they got used to the new equipment!

The families on the ranch were always provided with jars of milk with cream on top, and as many fresh eggs as you could use. There was also an ample supply of beef, chicken, pork, and lamb, and turkeys for Thanksgiving and Christmas. When a family put a box on the porch of the creamery, located near the vegetable garden, for the gardener to fill with seasonal vegetables, they might also be surprised with fresh flowers cut from the lovely flower gardens of Ridgewood.

We ranch children had the run of this big paradise of a ranch. We could hike or ride anywhere, using the Ridgewood horses and saddles. We could go see any of the beautiful Thoroughbred mares or handsome stallions any time, or watch the yearlings playing in the field. We were welcome to ride through the special Howard orchard with a wide variety of fruit and nuts, and help ourselves to the delicious fruit from the backs of our horses. We were invited to swim in their private pool. We could go to The Lake and the boathouse at anytime. Marcela always distributed lovely Christmas gifts to the children of each family, purchased from the nicest stores in the city. Sweater and skirt sets, nice western shirts, and whatever she thought we would use and enjoy. The Howards were very caring people, generous and kind to everyone, helping out anyone who needed it.

When Mr. Howard lost his son due to a tragic accident that happened on his beloved Ridgewood Ranch, he turned his unfathomable grief into something positive. He turned his time, energy, and generous amounts of money into building the Frank R. Howard Memorial Hospital in Willits, on a hill at the south edge of town overlooking the main street. This much needed hospital, planned by two men of vision, Doc Babcock and Mr. Howard, completed in 1928, had the latest and best equipment that could be purchased. The community wanted to help with the hospital project, too. The local businessmen got together and organized the Willits Frontier Days Celebration Parade and Rodeo held annually on July 4th. The proceeds from these several days of the Independence Day activities went toward furnishing the hospital with whatever the ongoing needs might be. Mr. Howard continued to help, too, sending the produce, meat, and dairy products from Ridgewood into town for use at the hospital. He continued to support and to have an interest in the Howard Hospital for the rest of his life. He will always be remembered in the Willits community for this generous act. Charles and Marcela will always be remembered for their zest for life, their great contributions and help with charitable projects, and to the world of horseracing, especially for bringing out the best in their special horse Seabiscuit. They created an excitement in the sport of horseracing in this country that has remained in the minds and hearts of America for a long, long time.

Ridgewood Ranch Aerial 1948

A

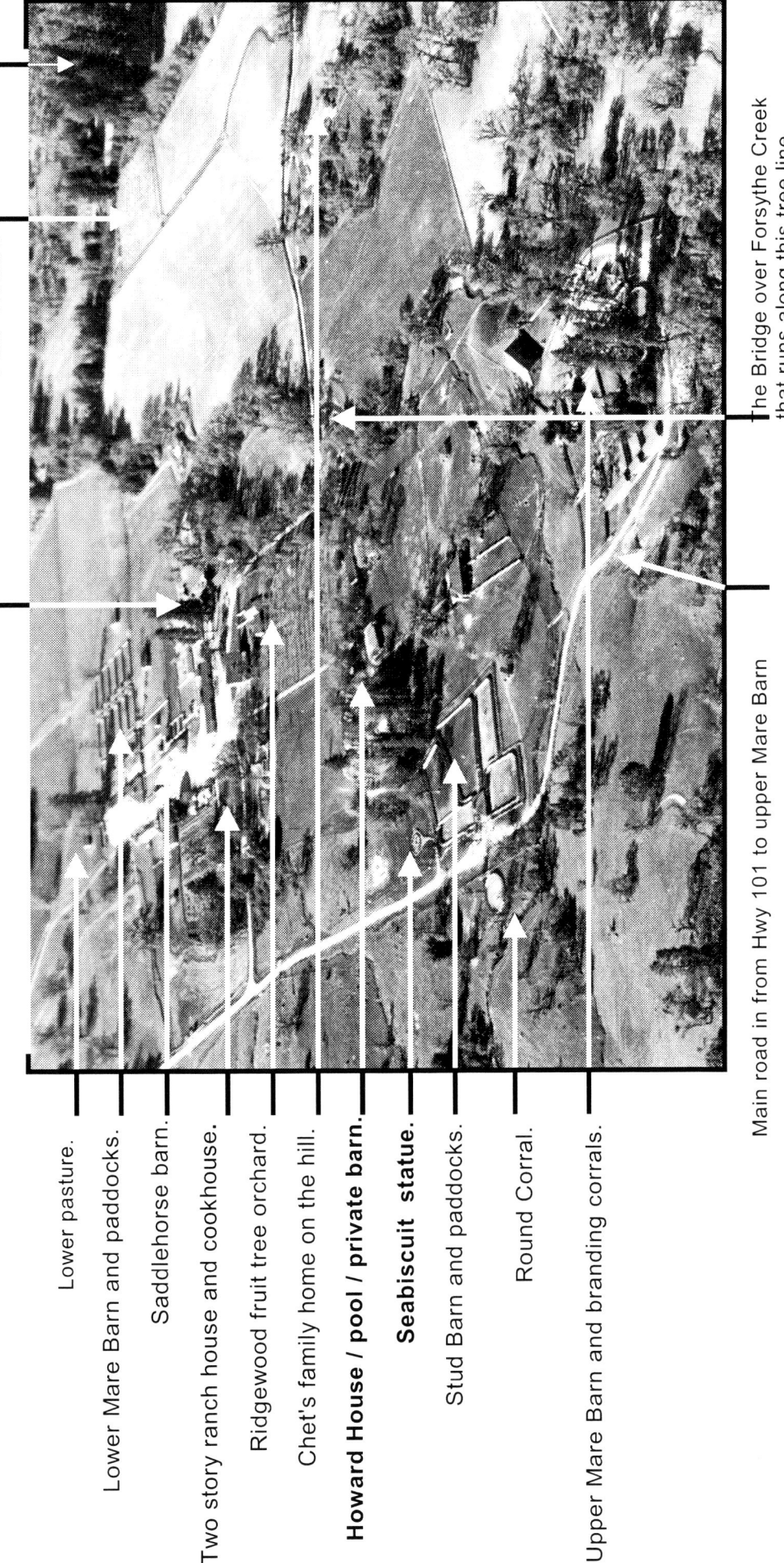

Ridgewood Aerial Photo with description of facilities

Copyright © Jani Buron 2002

Childhood memories sweet and clear

Bring back a happy yester-year

Words by the author Jani Buron 2002

Copyright © Jani Buron 2002

Copyright © Jani Buron 2002

This was the very familiar Ridgewood Ranch main entry gate off Highway #101 (The Redwood Highway). It was at the bottom of the Ridgewood Grade where this road led into Ridgewood Ranch. A little ways in, a left fork went to the main ranch headquarters, and the right road led visitors to the Stud Barn. The little sign to the left of the gate has the times and days of visitor hours. The redwood archway gate is no longer there, but the road is still in the same place. The main entry to the Ridgewood Ranch today is further north off Highway #101.

Copyright © Jani Buron 2002

This town truck delivered milk, meat, produce, and vegetables to the Howard Memorial Hospital that Mr. Howard built in memory of his son, Frankie, who perished in an auto accident on the Ranch in 1926. The truck also delivered the ranch children to school, and picked up the mail and newspapers, groceries, machinery parts, and delivered them back to the ranch families. Notice "Ridgewood Ranch" painted on the door, and the old California license plates.

Copyright © Jani Buron 2002

This is the beautiful Stud Horse Barn where visitors came to see Seabiscuit in his retirement years, as well the other famous Howard stallions. The barn was painted red and white like the C. S. Howard stable racing colors. The Triangle "H" brand, (used on the Howard racing colors), is prominently painted above the front door entrance, and on the colors of little jockey statues by the front door. (The Ridgewood Ranch brand for ranch livestock was a Quarter Circle "H".) The barn was always kept shiny and spiffy to receive the visitors from all over the world who came to see Seabiscuit and the other top Howard stallions.

The visitors guestbook table can be seen on the left inside the front door, where so many visitors came from around the world and stood to sign their names. It was always interesting to read the book's recent entries, and to see all the different states and countries that these people came from.

To us, as young girls, it seemed like even the neighboring states were very far away, let alone New York City or France! Marcela, (Mrs. Howard) would come and take the older pages from the book as it got full, read them, and then file them away.

The barnyard was always kept very neat, and had flowers and greenery all around it. During the summer's intense heat, the Ridgewood visitors seemed to linger a little longer under big spreading oak trees in front of the barn that provided shade for the parking area. They would converse with each other, or have some lunch or snacks they brought with them, before heading back out to Highway 101 to continue their journey. Ridgewood was located exactly halfway between the towns of Willits and Ukiah, being about 10 miles to either town. In the 1940's on the narrow two lane highway, it could take a while to get to either town, especially if it was north up the steep twisty Ridgewood Grade to Willits.

Once inside the barn, the visitors walked across the cool red-brick floors of the barn center, and past the inside corners of each of the four stalls. Each stall had an open-air window to the inside of the barn, so the horses could be observed at all times. Each stall opened to the outside into an individual paddock for each stallion.

Once outside the back of the barn, the visitors could see Seabiscuit's paddock on the left in the back, the one that was located closest to the Howard's Big House. And the people that came there also got to hear the Stud Barn host, Sarge, tell his stories about the horses and the Ranch and his other adventures as he ushered them around. And he had as many interesting stories as you had time. He guided visitors through the barn out to the paddock area where they could walk up on a little raised platform to observe the stallions. Most of the stallions liked to show off for the public, shaking their heads proudly and prancing around as the cameras clicked while people ooohed and ahhhed. Sarge even had Mioland trained to rear up on command. But the famous horse with the courageous heart, Seabiscuit, preferred to nap, or to stand quietly in his favorite corner and look at the people from some distance. Some visitors even asked, "Is that really Seabiscuit?" But his adoring public still loved him, and would return again and again to see him, because he was a very special horse with a very special spirit.

Later, after Seabiscuit died, the visitors who came to see the other Ridgewood stallions would walk out to gaze at Seabiscuit's remarkably crafted statue. They went out in back past the paddocks to the little walking ring that encircled this memorial tribute.

Flowers were planted all around the base of the statue, and shrubbery adorned the area as well. It was a very quiet peaceful place, located between the Howard house and the Stud Barn. And yet when you stood there and looked at the likeness of The Biscuit who was gazing off into the distance, instead of the presence of country quiet, you could almost hear the racing crowds in the grandstand cheering him on to another dazzling victory. How they enjoyed seeing him run! What a tremendous display of continuous courage, wit, intelligence, perseverance and thrilling speed he displayed! How fortunate were those who witnessed this unforgettable horse perform during his racing days.

Copyright © Jani Buron 2002

Sea Sovereign was one of Seabiscuit's more famous offspring. He was known as "the best son of the immortal Seabiscuit". He raced successfully at age 2 and 3, then was retired due to injury. He bore a great resemblance in appearance to his famous father.

During his career he won the Santa Catalina Handicap, and was second in the San Vicente Handicap, and won an allowance race. Altogether, he had 8 starts, including 3 wins and 2 seconds.

Copyright © Jani Buron 2002

This is Seabiscuit's statue and Tex Wheeler, the man who created it.

Copyright © Jani Buron 2002

This ranch colt out for daily exercise seems startled to see that big horse on the pedestal looking at him!

Copyright © Jani Buron 2002

Sarge and Ajax in the paddock at the Stud Barn, 1948. Ajax was bred and raced in Australia, and he won 36 of his 46 starts, and was unplaced only once. He finished 2nd seven times, and 3rd twice. He won 18 consecutive races, a proud accomplishment for any horse.

Copyright © Jani Buron 2002

This is Sabu, son of Mahmoud. Sabu was the sire of Sabu Rock, who raced and broke records at Northern California racetracks. Sabu Rock was owned and trained by Chet Griffith.

Copyright © Jani Buron 2002

Mioland performing for Sarge in the Stud Barn Paddock, 1948.
Mioland was the winner of 11 stakes races, and ran second in the Preakness, and third in the Hollywood gold Cup. He raced from age 2 through 6.

Copyright © Jani Buron 2002

Ajax enjoying the Ridgewood sunshine at the Stud Barn, Summer of 1948.

Copyright © Jani Buron 2002

Chet, on the left, and Sarge at the horse's head, are in the yard in front of the Stud Barn. The new round corral is in the background. That is where the stud horses were exercised sometimes instead of doing a walk around the ranch.

Copyright © Jani Buron 2002

This crop of Ridgewood yearlings is enjoying the lush green pastures and the shade of the oak trees.

Copyright © Jani Buron 2002

(Left photo) This is at the Wager place roundup corrals, on Reeves Canyon Road, at the southern end of the Ridgewood Ranch property. It is off Highway #101 a few miles south of the Ridgewood Ranch gate. Ray Kane, ranch foreman, is taking a break here between the marking and branding activity. While Ray was foreman, the roundups were done here at the Wager place, then in later years they were done in the corrals at the Upper Mare Barn.

(Right photo) These Wager corrals of split-rail fencing were partly on a hillside, and part on the flat. There was a little shady creek that ran through the place, and even on the hottest days, it was cool down there. Those of us that were too young to be roping in the corrals played in the creek most of the day, wading and catching pollywogs and digging deeper wading ponds! The ice-filled tubs of soda and beer were set down in the running creek where they kept cool all day. The Orange Crush soda in the little brown ribbed glass bottles was a favorite with us kids.

Ray Kane is on the dark horse in the foreground. As you can see, men and women both pitched in to get the job done.

Copyright © Jani Buron 2002

Copyright © Jani Buron 2002

Lots of help always showed up at these roundups; neighboring ranch hands and friends, people from town, and families from far away who made a special trip for it. It was really quite an exciting day, sometimes two, getting all the work done on the cows and calves. Everyone enjoyed the great meals with the thick steaks, campfire barbecued (Ridgewood beef, of course); and the visiting, and the stories that were told; it was all a part of the whole gathering.

Back row, left to right: The Ridgewood horse Tick-Tock, (pictured with Tom Smith in Laura Hillenbrand's "Seabiscuit" book on pg. 18, when he was a racetrack pony-horse for the Howard racing stable.) , Laverne on the ground next to Tick Tock, and other familiar faces.

Front row, left to right: Jeff Albee with my little brother, Alma Albee, and further to the right, Jani, standing, and Betty kneeling by her Dad, Curly.

Copyright © Jani Buron 2002

Some more of the Wager roundup crew from the opposite end. Front row, from left to right: Jeff Albee, standing, with John, Jani standing next to Laverne, and down on the right end, Florence Persico holding Chuck, with Lee standing in front. Lots of familiar faces of riders on the horses in the back row.

Copyright © Jani Buron 2002

Above are a few more horses and riders at the Wager roundup. From left to right: Tick Tock's head. The third and fourth people from the left are a striking couple, Don and Pitrita Coleman, from Hollywood, who owned the Mill Iron ranch in Willits. They were at most of our gatherings, and always rode in the Willits Frontier Days July 4th Parade.

Many celebrities who were friends of the Howards came to the ranch, including some pretty famous movie stars. To us, they were just very nice people who were there to see the horses and visit with the Howards. We did not get autographs or photos, because it did not stand out in our minds that they were so famous. It was just an ordinary happening to see them about the Ranch. We knew that we were not supposed to use the Howard swimming pool if we knew they were entertaining guests, but there were even exceptions to that rule. We walked up there on one hot summer day in our swimsuits with a beach towel around our shoulders, and unexpectedly found guests at the pool. Instead of turning us away, they politely asked us to come on in.

Copyright © Jani Buron 2002

These smiling faces are more of the families that came to the 1945 Wager roundup. Doesn't everyone look happy? In the very front row, seated, are Laverne, with braids; Lee Persico; and Jani, brushing some corral dust from her eye. Betty is standing up to the right of Jani, balancing on one foot, showing us her new western boots! Betty is looking toward Dink Persico, and Florence Persico holding baby Chuck. Ray Kane is standing in back on the far left.

The day is over, the chores are done. The working crew came early in the morning to do the separating, marking and branding. Some of the Grandmas, and other women with the younger babies came out later in the day and brought the rest of the food. And what a spread there was of home-cooked bread, beans, side dishes and desserts! The aroma of that food in the outdoors, mixed with the barbecue smoke of the big cooking on the fire would make anyone hungry.

After a day out in the sun, how welcome the get-together was under the trees, with friends and lively conversation and cool drinks and good food. Then came the best part, the reminiscing around the glowing campfire coals after the meal was consumed. At each branding time, there were new stories to be told and old ones to be re-told, and the ritual of a remembering time for those who had passed on since the last gathering. This reminiscing is how the younger ones learned of times past, and to some those memories became very dear.

At left, ranch foreman Ray Kane and Petie Coleman, in the chow line after the 1945 Wager marking and branding at Ridgewood.

Copyright © Jani Buron 2002

At right, some of the Persico family tailgaiting it for lunch. Standing is Lee, seated is his mom, Florence, and inside is his brother, Chuck, and a little friend to the right.

Copyright © Jani Buron 2002

Copyright © Jani Buron 2002

These three little girls are upstairs on the veranda of the grand old Willits Hotel, watching the Willits Frontier Days Rodeo Parade go by on Main Street. Jani is in the middle, and the Pippin sisters are on either side. Jani's Grandfather, who lived in Laytonville, had a permanent room at the Willits Hotel. He kept it for family to stay in when we were in town, or when he was there. During Frontier Days, we came to town from the ranch and stayed there day and night for the whole event. What a fun celebration it was, picnicking in the hotel rooms, with parade, rodeo, carnival, dances, and barbecues to go to. Nonstop fun for kids!

Copyright © Jani Buron 2002

This is a July 4th parade going south on Main Street in Willits. The two story building across the street with the decorative corner windows was the Purity Store on the street level, and upstairs was Doc Babcock's office.

Copyright © Jani Buron 2002

This is the statue of Seabiscuit in 1949, done by Tex Wheeler. It was put up at Ridgewood Ranch out near the Stud Barn after Seabiscuit had passed away. Another statue identical to this one, is at the Santa Anita racetrack entrance to the grandstand across from the George Woolf memorial statue. Many Ridgewood visitors came out and walked around The Biscuit's likeness here at the ranch, remembering his glory days of racing. The Howard house is in back of the tall trees in the background.

Below is a view of the statue from the other side, with the road to the Stud Barn going by the fenceline in back of it. 1949.

Copyright © Jani Buron 2002

Copyright © Jani Buron 2002

Jani on Billy The Kid ,and a ranch hand, Jim, on a horse he was breaking, resting in front of the Stud Barn.

Copyright © Jani Buron 2002

Jani is on Billy here, standing in the yard where the road led up to the Stud Barn. This whole area would often be filled with the parked cars of the visitors who came to see Seabiscuit. The visitors would patiently wait their turn to go in and see the famous stallions of Ridgewood. They enjoyed the ranch atmosphere, and taking in all the lush green pastures and shady trees and mountain scenery surrounding them.

Copyright © Jani Buron 2002

Laverne, Jani, and Betty on Betty's little pumpkin-colored horse, Doonie, under the big spreading oak tree in front of the Ridgewood Stud Barn. We were being silly this day, trying to look like true mountain girls with the bare feet, rolled up jeans, and only a rope around Doonie's nose instead of a bridle. Doonie is the only one not smiling!

We three had a lot of good rides and hikes, and spent many happy hours together. Laverne and Betty are sisters, and their family treated me like a sister, too. Laverne was the "Big Sister" to both of us younger ones, kind of keeping a watchful eye over us. That bond of being a "Ridgewood Kid" still keeps us close today, many, many years later.

Copyright © Jani Buron 2002

    This was taken in the main Ridgewood Ranch headquarters yard, in front of the saddle horse barn. The cookhouse, the creamery, and the ranch foreman's two-story house behind the trees are unseen, across the road. The girls are by the hitching rail near the saddle horse barn, getting ready to go for a ride. Betty is on Charro, and Jani is on Tick Tock, who was a racetrack pony-horse for the Howard racing stable, that Seabiscuit's trainer Tom Smith rode. At Ridgewood, Mr. Howard also rode Tick Tock as a pony-horse to accompany Seabiscuit and Red Pollard during their daily exercise around Ridgewood, while preparing Seabiscuit to return to the racetrack. Both Red and The Biscuit were recuperating from serious racetrack injuries, and slowly exercising their way back to health together.

Copyright © Jani Buron 2002

This is the Ridgewood Ranch Saddle Horse Barn, with the cement watering trough and hitching rail out in front. The barn had a nice large tack room and many roomy stalls, and a large hayloft where we pushed feed down into the mangers for the horses. The barn was kept very clean, as were all the barns on the Ranch. We were welcome to use any of the horses or saddles from that barn, knowing that we were to put both away cleaner than we found them.

One of our chores was to regularly clean that big cement water trough next to the hitching rail. First we had to remove the large wooden plug, or bung, from it, which always took some pounding and some doing because it swelled up from being in the water. Then as the water drained out, we scrubbed off the moss from the sides and bottom, then emptied it out good and rinsed it again. Only after someone inspected it for clean, was it ready to refill. We also learned to clean the stalls of the horses we used, and to clean and soap the saddles and tack, and to sweep out the tack room often, keeping it neat and tidy.

Copyright © Jani Buron 2002

This is Betty and Doonie in 1949, in the middle of the headquarters barnyard. The saddle horse barn is in the back, and the Lower Mare Barn is beyond it by the tall pine trees.

Copyright © Jani Buron 2002

This is the Ridgewood Ranch bunkhouse, located in the main ranch compound between the cookhouse and the Lower Mare Barn. The single ranch hands stayed here, and they ate at the cookhouse. We girls were told to keep our distance from here, lest we overhear a cussword or a colorful story not meant for our young ears! The other ranch hands with families each had their own homes, located on various parts of the ranch.

These gardens all around the drive-way leading up to the Howard's Ridgewood home were filled with exotic, colorful, beautiful flowers, shrubs, and trees at all times. Norman, the gardener, kept the place immaculate. He lived in a little cottage on these grounds. The Howard house was actually hidden from view with the greenery. Today the house is clearly visible from the road.

To the right is another view of the Gardens around the Howard estate

This swimming pool was located in the Howard House side-yard. It was an elegant pool with a low dive and a high dive, a nice bathhouse, and pretty lamppost lights. Mrs. Howard saw us swimming in the creek one day, and generously invited us to use their pool anytime that they were not using it.

What a deal! It was so pretty, and so clean and blue colored, and such a nice place to spend the long hours of a hot summer day. But we still enjoyed our creek swimming holes, too, when we were out riding in the summertime. We truly had the best of both worlds!

To the left: The road going down hill in the foreground is from our house down to the road to the lake. Lion Mountain, named for its large mountain lion population, is the prominent forested hill in the background.

Below is the lake Mr. Howard built after he purchased the Ranch. He built a nice boathouse on it that is to the right and just out of this photo. He had several kinds of boats there, including a bicycle boat, (early in life, he had been a bicycle repairman.)

Around the boathouse was a nice place where we swam. The lake is called Walker Lake, built on Walker Creek, and the valley that the main part of Ridgewood Ranch is built in is the Walker Valley.

Copyright © Jani Buron 2002

Here is Sea Sovereign, son of Seabiscuit, out for a walk, with Hubert on his back. Chet and Billy The Kid are going along, too.

Copyright © Jani Buron 2002

Hubert Jones is exercising Sabu at Ridgewood. Chet is with him on Billy the Kid. The stud horses were exercised regularly and always seemed to enjoy their outings around the ranch. The new home that Mr. Howard had built for the Griffith family is on the hill in the background. Taken in 1949.

This is the house on the hill that the Howard's built for our family as an incentive for my Dad to come back to work for them for a second time, and be in charge of all the Thoroughbred horses on Ridgewood. Mrs. Howard asked my Mom if there was any special feature she would like in the house, and Mom said "a sun room", and it was done! You can see the big windows on the right where the morning sun came in so warm. It was one of our favorite places during the cold weather. This house was roomy and new and well built; what fun it was to move in there! The view from all sides across the fields to the far hills was spectacular. The best thing was that I could keep my horse, Billy The Kid, in the closest field below the house. He usually had the great big pasture all to himself. I could just go down to see him and sit in the apple tree and feed him apples, or go for a ride anytime I wanted to, unless, of course, it was school time!

This is Jani's Mom, Iny outside by the sunroom of the new house on a Summer day in 1949.

Copyright © Jani Buron 2002

This was taken on a Spring morning in 1950, just as Jani was leaving for school. She is standing by the Chevy panel truck which served as the Ridgewood school bus. The regular school district bus would not travel the narrow, steep, and dangerous Ridgewood Grade on the old Hwy 101, either up or down, so the ranch provided us with transportation to school in the morning, and our folks picked us up at the Forestry Station at the top of the Grade where the regular school bus left us off in the afternoon.

The fellow driving the Ridgewood bus also picked up any shopping lists anyone had for town, and he brought back the mail and the paper from town, and picked up whatever the ranch needed in the way of parts and supplies.

Sometimes at the Forestry in the afternoon, we girls would have a little wait for our folks to get there. We waited outdoors, sitting on the little low rock wall that bordered the Forestry yard, talking or doing homework. Sometimes we devised different outdoor games to pass the time. The Forestry had built a beautiful, tall stone retaining wall slanted against one hill that was across the yard from the low rock wall. We would get back, run fast, and see who could jump up and touch to the highest rock on that wall. We did this over and over to see who could jump the highest the most times. There were many discussions about whose foot or hand actually touched which highest rock! The stone wall itself was a work of art. Each large stone was laid individually, equally spaced, with cement around it to hold each in place on the wall.

The other older house on the hill is in back and to the right of the panel truck. It was still there, by itself, and occupied, when I went back in December of 2001.

Copyright © Jani Buron 2002

This 1950 picture is of Jani's kitty sitting on the cornerpost of the fence that was in front of both the old ranch house where Jani lived with the Jones family, and the new house built on the same spot for the Griffith family.(The cornerpost was still there in December of 2001 when I went back.)The Jones family moved down to the big two-story house connected to the cook- house in the main ranch compound. The old house was then torn down, and our new house was built in exactly the same place. The fields across the way are in the background, and are bordered by Lion Mountain.

The "new" house was eventually moved off the hill (quite a feat!) down to the main compound. It was needed there after the combination two-story house and ranch cookhouse burned down later, when the ranch was under new ownership. Our "new" house still stands in it's new location today.

A note about the kitty: She was my cat, and we named her Hooker because she had caught her tail in the screen door at some time, and it had a definite deviation, up and over and back where the door had slammed shut. It looked like a little hook. She used to come to the walkway under my bedroom window at nighttime, and meow so I would open the window and push the screen out so she could jump in, so she could, of course, sleep on the foot of my bed. On one particular cold night, she meowed to come in, then once in, meowed to go out, then meowed to come in again. After about the 3rd time of doing this, she wouldn't jump back up onto the window sill by herself, but just meowed even louder. I leaned out of the window to pick her up and bring her in so we could all get to sleep, and just as I deposited her on my bed, out popped a baby kitten! I called to my Mom for help, and we got a little box and lined it with a blanket and put it in the bathroom near the little heater, where Hooker had four more kittens on through the night and into the morning. She had not looked like she was carrying kittens, so this was quite a surprise!

Copyright © Janu Buron 2002

Jani had just saddled up Billy the Kid for a ride when her little brother John came out of the house and wanted to go for a short ride first. Her dog Laddie was ready to go, too. This was taken on a crisp fall day in the back yard of the Griffith home on the hill, right above the pasture where Billy The Kid was kept. The mountain peak way in the background is what we called "Big Rock Candy Mountain", and it is clearly visible from the top part of Ridgewood Grade on Hwy.#101, and is seen in the background of many photos taken from Ridgewood. We girls hiked up that peak often, taking flags and poles and putting them up, usually to replace the ones that had gone by the wayside during the previous winter. We could look across the deep canyon over to Highway 101 to the Ridgewood Grade, and wave to the people in the cars going by. Some waved back to us, and some looked so surprised to see three little girls up there on that little mountain top! Others were so busy concentrating on driving up or down that infamous Grade that they didn't even look in our direction.

Copyright © Jani Buron 2002

    This is some publicity in the form of an old-fashioned "hold-up" being staged to generate interest in the upcoming 1949 July 4th, Frontier Days Celebration Parade and Rodeo. We approached some visitors that had arrived from San Francisco, took them here in the buggy, had them step out and hold up their hands while we told them about the Frontier Days coming up in two weeks, and made them promise to be here for all the fun! Everyone had a good time doing this, even the supposed "victims"! Jani is on her brown and white pinto horse, Billy The Kid, on the right.

Copyright © Jani Buron 2002

This is the 1948 July 4th Willits Frontier Days Rodeo parade as it travels south down Main Street in Willits, California. The Ridgewood Ranch cowboys and cowgirls rode as a group, wearing Western straw hats and jeans, white shirts and red satin ties, representing the red and white colors of Howard's Ridgewood Ranch and racing stable colors. Left, Jani is on Billy The Kid, and next to her is Betty is on Doonie.

THE JULY 4TH WILLITS FRONTIER DAYS, PARADE, AND RODEO

The Willits Frontier Days Rodeo and Parade was a big hometown annual July 4th celebration, and it was always fun. We made plans and looked forward to it all year. My Dad helped put on the rodeo, along with everyone else, and for two years he was chairman of the rodeo committee. My Mom helped with the entries and rodeo secretary duties. At one time, the money made on Frontier days went to the Howard Hospital fund, and so Doc Babcock was a big supporter, too. Started in 1926 it was, and still is, a big event in Willits and all of Mendocino County, billed as the oldest continuous Rodeo in California. It is traditionally a two-day rodeo, but it had, on occasion, been a three-day event, years ago. The surrounding activities, of the Jr. Rodeo, and the carnival, were taking place all week. But the BIG day was the Fourth of July, with the parade, the big barbecue feed, and the rodeo.

It seems that everyone came to town for the rodeo, even a man known as The Hermit. We saw him for years never knew him by any other name. He would come out of the mountains into town, get into parade formation, and slowly ride his bicycle down Main Street in the parade, his long white beard and white hair flowing. He wore a kind of a buckskin robe outfit, and it always looked cleaned up some for the occasion. He had a fixed facial expression of a slight smile, but I never heard him talk. After the 4th of July, he disappeared, but we could count on seeing him again next year if he survived the winter. We never knew just where he lived in the hills. He was a memorable sight, gliding down Main Street on his bicycle, looking as though this was the highlight of his whole year.

Logging trucks were in the parade, too, each with their biggest and best redwood log to show off. These logs were so huge that they made the big trucks look small. The logs were safely fastened to the bed of the truck trailer with big heavy chains. Sometimes it took three trucks to haul one tree log, each carrying one portion of a tree after it was cut into thirds.

Colorful floats, horse drawn and motor driven, were a part of the parade, along with lively bands, and marching groups from all over the State, including military drill teams, and single entries of a horse and rider. The Willits city fire engines and Forestry fire engines led the parade, followed by the Grand Marshall and various dignitaries.

Most ranches rode as groups in the parade, and Ridgewood was one of the biggest. We had lots of riders, and the stagecoach drawn by a fine team of horses. All the horses were bathed and their coats were oiled and their hooves were polished. The saddles and bridles were soaped and shined up. We were a fine looking group!

After the parade went down Main Street, to the enjoyment of large enthusiastic crowds, we turned down a small dirt street that came into the side of the rodeo grounds. Once there, we stayed in formation and rode past the grandstand on the racetrack for those who preferred to sit in one place to view both the parade and the rodeo. They were always appreciative, and clapped and cheered for us as we went by.

After the parade, we took our horses over to the cool oak tree grove in back of the grandstand, where we watered them, loosened up the saddle cinches, and then tied them up in the shade. Then we went for a hamburger and an ice-cold soda at one of the concession booths under the backside of the grandstand. Then it was rodeo time!

There was a racetrack around the outside of the rodeo arena and stock pen complex in those years, and there was activity going on all the time, in any direction you looked. Some events that took place on the track right in front of the grandstand were trail horse competition, color horse classes, stake races, the clown acts, and at some point during the rodeo, trick riding. In the arena, cowboys and cowgirls competed in bronc riding, calf roping, barrel racing, bull riding, team roping, and bulldogging, or steer wrestling.

About three times during each rodeo performance, open horse races were held around that oval, with a lap and tap start. Now that was exciting, just getting the horses all facing in one direction and having all the horses and jockeys ready for the start at the same time. Ready or not, the starting gun sounds, and the rodeo announcer says, "They're off!". Usually in a cloud of dust, I might add! Three races per day was the usual card, and the same horses could compete in any or all of the races they could handle. Some horses had lots of stamina, but they also had to be able to handle the sharp turns of the small track. And racing luck was racing luck, so even if you bet with someone on a sure thing, it might not happen! But you had a three-day go at it, so there was always next time. It was a lot of excitement for the crowd at Willits.

Sometime during each rodeo performance, the Persico family of Willits entertained the crowd with rope tricks, and trick riding. Their oldest son, Lee, was billed as the "World's Youngest Trick Rider", and the audience always looked forward to seeing him perform. So he could not goof off with the rest of us kids, because he watched close to see when his time was to go out on the track and do the tricks with his horse. Then, after he was done with the act, he could rip around with the rest of us between the carnival and the rodeo grounds. To keep cool all day, we drank lots of ice cold Orange Crushes. The sweet, wholesome taste out of the glass bottle was unlike any of today's soda pops. We did check in with our folks once in a while, so they knew where to find us.

The whole town celebrated Frontier Days with decorated windows, various July 4th events, parties and get-togethers. It seemed like the community partied all day and all night. Some fellas even rode their horse into the saloons to order a drink, saying that there was no place to tie their horse up outside. They were served.

There were two hotels in town, right across a sidestreet from each other, both on a corner facing Main Street. One was the Willits Hotel, where my Grampa lived, and the other was the Hotel Van. Both were grand in their own way. And there was not a hotel room to be had in town, because we all came in from the ranches and got rooms to stay in town for the whole Frontier Days festival. The women brought a good supply of homemade food to the rooms with them, so there was never a shortage of something to eat back at your family's room. It was fun to eat with another family, too, to see what kind of treats they had. The carnival was so much fun, so colorful at night with all the rides and games that we only saw once a year!

At one July 4th Rodeo, when my Dad was rodeo chairman and my Mom was doing secretary duties in the grandstand, there was an especially exciting event. The Monty Montana trick riding family had come to entertain rodeo-goers. Monty's claim to fame was a well-done four-horse catch. I had not seen this done before. In the four-horse catch, he stood on the ground and threw his large rope loop around four galloping horses as they passed by him. Not much margin for error in this one.

Monty and my Dad were friends, and, unknown to me, or my Mom, they had arranged earlier for me to be one of the four riders in that four-horse loop! Monty came up to me and introduced himself to me while I was watering my horse at the oak tree where I had tied him. Monty said he had watched me ride, asked me if I would like to be in the four-horse catch, and if I thought my horse and I could do the ride. I was surprised...all these other riders around, and he wants me? Eleven year old me? I said I would have to go find my Dad and ask him. Monty said he had already gotten permission from Dad, and Monty was short one rider, and the act was going on soon. So I tightened up the cinch, checked my saddle, mounted up and rode by and caught Dad's eye and got an OK. Then I went quickly to do a couple of practice runs with the other three to get a feel for staying together in line straight across the track with them. Me, riding with the trick riders! Thoughts raced through my head of the times when I used to pretend to be a trick rider at home, with my little horse Billy the Kid being very patient with me and my saddle acrobatics. So we practiced for a few minutes, Monty's family and I, and then they signaled it was time to do it for real. They said, "Just ride at an even pace, and when the loop comes over you, just keep going at the same measured pace".

We four started out galloping easy, stayed even, turned our faces toward the grandstand and smiled at the crowd, and galloped past Monty. He threw a perfect loop around us as we went by. My horse went at just the right speed, and we all four passed through the huge loop Monty had thrown. It was fun!

The crowd loved it. But my Mom didn't know that it was I riding in that four-horse catch until the announcer said, "here comes the Monty Montana family and Janet Griffith of Willits for the four-horse catch!" Dad, who did know, was busy running the Rodeo and hadn't gotten word to her, and she was busy with the rodeo secretary papers down in a front booth in the grandstand. She looked up, then stood up when she heard my name called, just in time to see me riding with the group. Her rodeo secretary papers went flying. She grabbed her camera and clicked it just a spectator stood up in front of her, and she got a picture of the back of his head instead of me in the four-horse catch. She was so surprised because she didn't know I was riding in the act, but she was excited and happy! And was I happy! What a wonderful memory of that day!

Photo by Larry Melious of The Dark Room, Willits, California

Copyright © Jani Buron 2002

These cows have been gathered and brought in from furthermost hills around Ridgewood Ranch, in preparation for the spring marking and branding. Each group of riders took a different corner of the ranch to bring the cows in from everywhere. It was a long day's work, starting before sun-up. It was usually almost sundown by the time we got close to the ranch headquarters. By this time, all horses, cows, dogs, and people were ready to call it a day. This photo was taken as we were going past on the road below the Griffith house on the hill.

The third rider out from the fence in the back on the light colored horse is Jani's Dad, Chet; to the right on the white pinto horse, Billy The Kid, is Jani, and next to her on the dark horse, Charro, is Laverne. The rider ahead of Laverne is her Dad, Curly, followed by a ranch cow-dog.

The cows have moved on further, getting closer to home.

The cows are approaching the bridge that spans Forsythe Creek that runs through the ranch. Then they will make a right turn just past the bridge and go up into the ranch headquarters yard, then on to the Upper Mare Barn corrals where they will be turned out and fed and watered to await the excitement of marking and branding day.

Chet and Bud "shooting the breeze" by the fence at the Upper Mare Barn.

The marking and branding crew standing around the early morning branding-iron fire waiting for the action to begin. Dink Persico is in the left foreground. In the far background beyond the fence is the familiar square roof of the Stud Barn surrounded by oak trees.

Copyright © Jani Buron 2002

Here we're moving the mother cows and calves to the next corral, at the 1949 Ridgewood spring branding.

Copyright © Jani Buron 2002

Jani, age 11, on her horse Billy The Kid, holding cows in the corner of the corral under the shade of the tall pines at the Ridgewood Upper Mare Barn during the Spring 1949 marking and branding.

In the previous photo, just over the fence behind the cows you can see the livestock weighing scale, one of the most modern of that time, and it still appears to be in working condition today. We used to have fun putting our horses into the little roofed and fenced structure with the spring loaded floor, then close the gate, and go outside and add the brass weights to the scale apparatus and then slide the heavyweight along the numbers on the scale until we got an accurate number of pounds registered for the horse. Then one of us would get in there, and the other girl outside would see what the horse plus the girl inside weighed! Then we would add a dog or two, and so on, until we knew what everything walking nearby weighed.

Seabiscuit was weighed on this scale, too, while reducing to racing weight and undergoing light training at Ridgewood prior to his return to the racetrack. He loved to eat, and had to be put on a strict diet in order to get back to his slim and trim training weight.

Part of the Upper Mare Barn is in the background on the right side, and on the roof you can see the windows to the upstairs apartments. Mrs. Howard had one of these apartments refurbished for our family to live in while our new house was being built. It was fun living there at the barn, hearing the horses soft nighttime noises coming from their stalls below. I kept my horse right outside in the corral below my bedroom window, and it was very handy to go riding. While I was living there, I also raised a little abandoned fawn one of the ranch hands brought to me. We named him "Bucky", and he was a fine pal, until he grew up one day and let it be known that he wanted *out* of that pen! We then returned him to the woods to join the resident deer herd.

Copyright © Jani Buron 2002

At left, Chet Griffith holding down the calf, while other Ranch help does the doctoring, marking and branding.

Below, Jani and Billy are helping separate the calves. The building over the fence at the end of the Upper Mare Barn was the breeding barn at one time, and then it was refurbished to accommodate some very modern and sophisticated veterinary equipment, such as a large horse examining table with bright lights over it, and X-ray machines.

Copyright © Jani Buron 2002

Left: Here are some of the kids sitting in the shade on the fence watching the marking and branding action in the corral. These gatherings were always especially fun for us kids, because that is when we got to work, visit, and play with the neighboring ranch children. There was always a lot of activity to watch, and plenty of cold sodas for us in the ice tub, and a spread of food put out that was delightful.

Below: These men are placing the famous Quarter Circle H brand on this little calf, a process that they will repeat throughout the day, until all the Howard cattle in these corrals are looked over, identified, doctored, marked, and branded.

Copyright © Jani Buron 2002

Some of the women worked hard in the corrals, and some brought food, and some did both. They always seemed to enjoy visiting and exchanging stories about their families and friends and activities, and catching up on the latest community news.

Copyright © Jani Buron 2002

The ranch crew in fast action with these two.
Iny is up on the fence observing.

Ted, Monte, and Hooper, the ranch carpenter, sitting on the fence watching the branding at Ridgewood, 1949.

Chet Griffith watching the three man calf crew in action, and Betty on Charro and Jani on Billy the Kid going after more calves.

Dust flies as the crew gets another calf down to doctor.

Little cowboy Johnny, friend Bud, and Pat, in the corrals at the Ridgewood 1949 marking and branding.

Left: These Ridgewood Ranch kids have a good vantagepoint to watch the marking and branding of 1949. Left to right: Brothers Mike and Johnny, and my brother John.

Right: Hubert Jones, on the left, was Laverne and Betty's older brother. Because of his light weight and good horsemanship, Mr. Howard got permission from his folks to have Hubert as one of the jockeys for his racing stable. Hubert won a lot of races, and stayed in the racetrack business even after he quit riding. On the right, sitting on the fence, is Ray Kane, one of the Ridgewood Ranch foremen in the 1940's.

Copyright © Jani Buron 2002

Jani on Billy the Kid, pushing cows at the 1949 Ridgewood branding.

Copyright © Jani Buron 2002

The crew brands another calf at the Ridgewood spring branding, 1949. Iny watches from the fence, Dink stands by fence below.

My Dad Chet is relaxing here, the day is almost done.

Copyright © Jani Buron 2002

Dink Persico roping on his palomino. Chet and Dink and their families were good friends of many years.

Copyright © Jani Buron 2002

Copyright © Jani Buron 2002

Pete catches one, and the crew goes to work.
Jani is on Billy going to bring some more calves around.

Copyright © Jani Buron 2002

Bobby on his horse Randy helping at the Ridgewood branding, 1949.

Copyright © Jani Buron 2002

Dust clouds being raised by working the cattle in the corrals consume the tall pine trees as the sun gets low at the close of the marking and branding day. To the right is Jani on Billy the Kid.

Jani and Billy The Kid getting ready to go riding.

Billy The Kid was a trick horse at Madison Square Garden in New York City before my Dad bought him, and eventually gave him to me. He knew how to do tricks, and trick riders rode him. He was a grand fellow, always travelling proud and showy, and yet so gentle with all of us. Notice that he doesn't have a halter on in some of these photos... he would follow me around and he didn't need a lead rope. In this picture he is "parking" for me (as in a show horse ring) as I give him the "park" voice command.

Copyright © Jani Buron 2000

Billy the Kid is "bowing" a thank you to his admirers, and going after the carrot Jani is giving him as a thank you. This was one of our favorite tricks. Buster dog is looking on.

Copyright © Jani Buron 2002

Jani and Betty are having fun with a very patient Billy The Kid. The dog Buster looks on, possibly thinking "All in a day's work, watching after these girls!"

Jani on Billy the Kid, and Betty on Blondie, on a June day in 1948.

Betty is on the fence watching Laverne feed Albert the Mule some hay. Ridgewood, 1946.

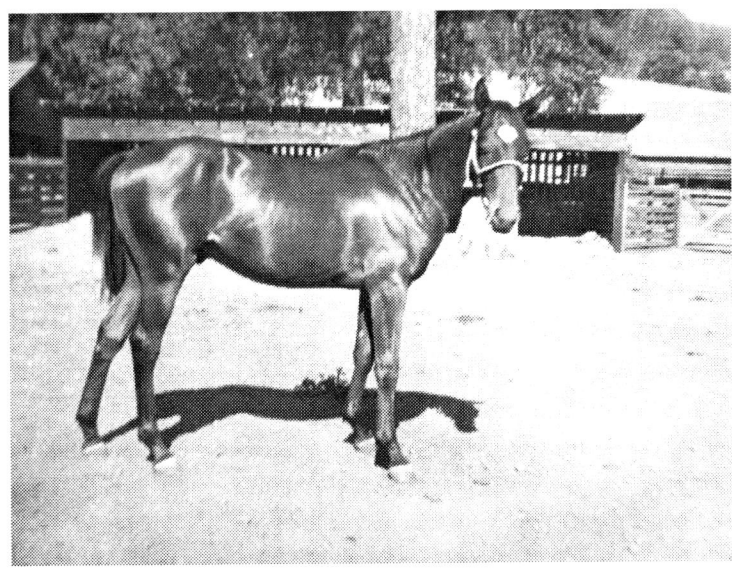
Copyright © Jani Buron 2002

This is one of the Mioland colts of the 1949 crop, as yet unnamed.

Copyright © Jani Buron 2002

    The foal on the right with this unusual blanket of spots was born of a Thoroughbred sire and dam, and was a very pretty little horse. Many people came to see this unusual baby, and by the age of three months the foal was sold for a fabulous price, making the Howards very proud. These two are enjoying the sunshine at the Lower Mare Barn, where all the Thoroughbred mares were taken to foal. In the daytime, each mare and foal were led out to their paddocks to play and exercise. Each night they were brought in to the coziness of their deeply bedded stalls.

I must say something about the Ridgewood snows that were so lovely. It was always a wonderful surprise when snows came to the valley. The big flakes floated down so softly, spinning this way and that. I do not remember anything like mountain blizzards and screaming winds happening here. Just the pretty, quiet, snowflakes drifting down from the steel gray clouds. As the snow began to stick, and build up, the evergreen landscape changed magically to a soft white sparkly wonderland. If it were cold enough for a long enough time, the shallow pond in the field below our house would freeze solid. Then we could "ice skate" around the pond on our shoes or boots that had the slickest soles. With snow on the ground all around the pond, it was really a Winter Wonderland!

Copyright © Jani Buron 2002

Snow came in many ways to the lovely hills of Ridgewood. If it snowed heavy enough, we would not have to go up the Ridgewood Grade to school, either because the Grade was deemed too dangerous to travel, or because in town the school was closed due to electricity being out. So when it started snowing, we cheered it on, hoping to get that wonderful day off school to go play in the snow. This scene is taken from the Griffith home on the hill, looking across the fields to the pear orchard with the small Redwood Grove standing behind it. It shows up much better in the snow than without, when all the tree greenery blends together.

Copyright © Jani Buron 2002

This is an especially pretty picture of the Ridgewood snow.

Copyright © Jani Buron 2002

This older house was there when I lived with the Jones family at Ridgewood. It sat in back of their house, and then later in back of the "new" Griffith house that was built later on the same spot. We remember the different families that lived there, and playing in their backyard on a big tire-on-a-rope swing that hung from a huge oak tree.

Copyright © Jani Buron 2002

Looking across the field to the snow-covered pear orchard.

Copyright © Jani Buron 2002

This was the view from the front window of our Ridgewood home, showing the same corner-post that the kitty is sitting on earlier in this book.

Copyright © Jani Buron 2002

Jani and "Snubby", a little lamb she made friends with at Ridgewood 1942.

Copyright © Jani Buron 2002

This cute little pair of pet racoons are in back of the Lower Mare Barn. The south end of the saddle horse barn is seen in the distance. 1942.

Copyright © Jani Buron 2002

Jani greeting the little Ridgewood bulldog on the lawn near the Stud Barn.

Copyright © Jani Buron 2002

This is Sabu, by Mahmood. Sabu is one of the studs who stood at Ridgewood.

Mr. Howard later gave my dad a parting gift of a stakes winning mare, Sag Rock, who was in foal to Sabu. We named that colt Sabu Rock. When we left Ridgewood in 1950, we went to the racetrack where my dad trained his own horses. Our horse, Sabu Rock, went on to win and set records at Northern California tracks, with my dad Chet as his owner and trainer. Ray Kane, a frequent visitor to Ridgewood Ranch, owned horses that my dad Chet trained. At the racetrack we saw many people that we had become aquainted with at Ridgewood. We also learned about the wonderful, exciting world of racing, and we were a part of it for many years.

Below is a win picture when Sabu Rock broke a track record at Pleasanton Fair. Sabu Rock ran at Tanforan Race Track and Bay Meadows. *Fourth from the left is the author, Jani, next to her is husband Vic holding daughter Vicki. Far left is brother John, next to Jani is Dolores and in the background is Jani's mother Iny. Far right is her father Chet.*

Copyright © Jani Buron 2002

This is the new six horse van my Dad purchased named "The Home Stretch Van", painted in silver letters on a dark blue body. There was a small living quarters in the back end, quite modern for it's day. We slept and ate in those living quarters while on trips of two or more days. We could feel and hear the horses moving around in the straw of their onboard stalls, and know that they were OK. Occasionally we would hear a soft nicker from one of them.

One of my first long trips outside of Mendocino County was with my Dad on that van, when we shipped some horses to Los Angeles. I got to go along as Dad's travelling partner so I could keep him awake while he was driving. I saw new sights, one of them being the broad flat expanse of the Central Valley of California. In some places where we were going down the Highway, I couldn't even see a mountain, no matter how hard I strained my eyes to the distant horizon. That was new to me, a land without mountains. It made me feel like I would fall off the edge of the horizon, if we ever reached that point. I was so busy looking at all the new country, that as the day went on into evening, I became very sleepy. I tried to sit up straight and stay alert and keep talking to Dad, but each time I nodded, and my forehead hit the dashboard, I knew I wasn't doing my part. He finally said, gently, "Jani, why don't you just lie down and take a nap." And I did. We stopped later at a wide spot alongside the highway to sleep for awhile, and to let the truck cool off some after climbing the steep Grapevine Grade.

Copyright © Jani Buron 2002

Early Ridgewood years: Jani, Dad and Mom by the oak tree at the Stud Barn.

Copyright © Jani Buron 2002

Last days at Ridgewood: My mom, Iny, and dad, Chet, Jani and John. 1950

A word here about Doc Babcock, who is an important player in the Ridgewood Ranch-Howard-Seabiscuit story. He was a vital part of the community because of and his friendship with Mr. Howard, and his inspiration of a much needed hospital that became a reality, and the medical care he gave to Red Pollard that enabled him to ride Seabiscuit into the winners circle again, his interest in Ridgewood, and his interest and support of Willits Frontier Days Parade and Rodeo, and all the wonderful and useful movie footage he took of the local history being made at that time.

To those of us who were his patients, we knew that he skillfully patched up, healed, advised, and chose the best and quickest path to recovery. He saved my Dad's life after he had been severely trampled by a crazed workhorse, and then hauled the 10 rugged miles to town to Howard Hospital. When my Mom was the victim of a raging life-threatening internal infection and needed something done immediately, the only two doctors in town heartily disagreed on the treatment she needed. She chose Doc Babcock's method, and it worked, and he brought her back to good health.

Doc took care of me at about age 5 when a case of bronchitis landed me in Howard Hospital. Then a couple of years later, while Mom and I were in a store doing school shopping in Willits, I suddenly felt weak, grew pale, and frightened the other ladies in the store when I fainted. Doc was summoned to the scene immediately. He promptly picked me up and carried me in his huge arms down Main Street, and diagonally across the intersection, stopping all traffic until we crossed. I remember him carrying me up the long steep stairs to his office, and puffing a little. He then gave me a thorough examination, and determined that I was only coming down with a severe case of the flu. He gave us instructions on how to minimize the discomforts, and sent us on our way. We were glad it was nothing worse and appreciated his quick attention.

Doc delivered my brother in a somewhat difficult birth. He was born just as the town's noon whistle was blowing, and he screamed along with it. He was then weighed in as the second heaviest baby ever born at Howard Hospital at that time. Chuck Persico held the top spot! The boys were born just months apart. Doc also stitched up my brother's face after an accident, and treated all his childhood ailments.

Doc Babcock was a good doctor, and intelligent man, and he had vision. He loved July 4th Frontier Days, and rode in the Parade, and took those great home movies that we are enjoying today. Thanks, Doc Babcock, where ever you are!

Copyright © Jani Buron 2002

The End !

EPILOGUE

I remember well the day in early 1950 that my parents called me in to the house and told me "We are leaving Ridgewood". I was devastated; it was like the bottom had fallen out of my world. I recall asking: "Why? Do we have to? Why can't we stay? " While I was churning inside, I tried to remain calm on the outside, not displaying the tumultuous feelings going on in my heart. I remember going outside and then down to the pasture and catching Billy up and going for a ride to think things over. Leaving Ridgewood? Why, I had never even thought of how to live anywhere else. Would I never see all these beautiful Thoroughbred horses again? And watch the newborn foals playing in the spring? And never be able to ride all these hills to my favorite spots? And not *live* here on the Ranch? It was too much for me to grasp all at once. And what about leaving Willits? What about all my friends? And school pals of many years?

In all the years I had been at Ridgewood, I had ridden or hiked to every corner of this huge 17,000 acre spread of a ranch. I knew the land as well as I knew the rooms inside of my house. All of the favorite places I had ridden to: the green fields, the creeks, the various outlying barns and pastures, the little family cemetery in the field, Big Rock Candy Mountain, Windy Gap, Eagle Peak, The Wager, The Martin, the covered reservoir, the mountaintop where the train tracks crossed, the patches of dark forests, the hillsides and canyons where the beautiful wildflowers grew, The Lake, the high points where you could see for miles across the ranch and beyond; we were going to be leaving all this?

Well, we did leave all of it. I did finish out my eighth grade school year at Willits High. On the last day of school, which was my 13th birthday, my folks arranged a grand surprise of a combination birthday-going away party with a picnic at the swimming hole on the river north of town. My friends and their families and some teachers attended, and everyone had such a good time. It was a wonderful day to remember.

And we did stay in Willits until after the Willits Frontier Days July 4th Rodeo, because my Dad was one of the directors, responsible for the whole rodeo that year, and my Mom was secretary. At the end of the summer, just one week before school started, we moved to Pleasanton, California; a new town, a new home, a new school, and I hoped new friends.

My Dad had always wanted to train his own thoroughbred racehorses, and it looked like now was the time. He had owned racehorses, but always had to hire a trainer at the track because he couldn't be there. Now, with the horse van he had (the "Home Stretch Van"), he could earn money hauling horses, and be able to train his own racehorses. The logical place to move to was Pleasanton, where one of the oldest and best racetracks in the country was located. That began a whole new part of my life, which is another story.

I became acquainted with the wonderful and exciting world of Thoroughbred racing, where Seabiscuit had been before coming back to Ridgewood, years earlier. I had only heard about the races, but had never been to one, other that the half-milers at the rodeos. They were open to anyone who thought he had the fastest horse of any kind. I had listened to all the Kentucky Derby races on the radio since the year Assault won in 1946, and I found that quite exciting. But, as I was about to find out, being there at the racetrack and having your own racehorses was even more of a thrill and adventure than listening to or watching the races. One of the greatest thrills of all time is when you experience your first trip to the winner's circle with your own horse! It is a day you remember forever.

I met and married my husband at the racetrack, and we worked our racing stable together. Our girls were part of it, too. Later on, we also took up the horse van business, using my Dad's Home Stretch Van. While we were training, Vic invented a horse bandage for one of our own horses, out of necessity. It became popular at racetracks across the country. We manufactured and sold them to distributors nationwide, and eventually we the moved the business to Nevada.

A word about my days at Ridgewood; All of us who lived there then were like one big family, because of the self-sufficient way of life that Mr. Howard provided on that Ranch. All the work done together, the social gatherings, and the close proximity of our homes, made us a closely-knit group. Today, people who are interested in learning more about the Ridgewood-Seabiscuit era will naturally have questions in their mind they want to ask about the people, events and happenings on the ranch. The loyalty to my "ranch family" of that time remains strong, and while I will answer most questions, there may be certain ones asked of me that will respectfully go unanswered.

Now, over 51 years hence, I have come back to Ridgewood for a visit. The present owners welcomed my initial visit very graciously, and invited us to look around at all parts of the ranch. It was both emotional, and gratifying, digging into past visually, and recounting the childhood memories. I have found that my feeling for this spot of ground that Ridgewood rests on, still draws me to it; I also found that Howard's grand large swimming pool seen as a child, had shrunk! I can handle the changes now; I have learned that you can remember a place like this that holds a special spot in your heart *both* ways: what *was*, and what *is*. I do very much enjoy the fact that so many people are once again interested in learning more about the special times of Seabiscuit and the Howard family at Ridgewood.

It is my fondest wish that by sharing my recollections and photos in this Ridgewood Ranch book, I have brought you a word picture of the sights, smells, and sounds of the happenings of those Ridgewood days. Perhaps this has given you an enjoyable glimpse into the past.

- Jani Buron -

L. Buron
P.O.Box 12
Wellington, NV 89444   **ORDER FORM**

Please send me _____ copies of Ridgewood Ranch of the 40's Book at $18.00 per copy, <u>Orders made on this form offer FREE shipping in the U.S.A</u> - Nevada residents add 7% tax - Mail this order to (S*hipping outside the U.S.A please inquire by mail.*)
Price good through 2005

_____
Name
_____
Address
_____
City   State   Zip   Phone

_____Check or Money order Enclosed (make check to **L.Buron**)

Signature_____

L. Buron
P.O. Box 12
Wellington, NV 89444

To:_____

Address:_____

City:_____

State:_____Zip_____

Mailing Label - Please Print

Include>Check, Order Form & mailing label

L. Buron
P.O.Box 12
Wellington, NV 89444   **ORDER FORM**

Please send me _____ copies of Ridgewood Ranch of the 40's Book at $18.00 per copy, <u>Orders made on this form offer FREE shipping in the U.S.A</u> - Nevada residents add 7% tax - Mail this order to (S*hipping outside the U.S.A please inquire by mail.*)
Price good through 2005

_____
Name
_____
Address
_____
City   State   Zip   Phone

_____Check or Money order Enclosed (make check to **L. Buron**)

Signature_____

L. Buron
P.O. Box 12
Wellington, NV 89444

To:_____

Address:_____

City:_____

State:_____Zip_____

Mailing Label - Please Print

Include>Check, Order Form & mailing label

L. Buron
P.O.Box 12
Wellington, NV 89444   **ORDER FORM**

Please send me _____ copies of Ridgewood Ranch of the 40's Book at $18.00 per copy, <u>Orders made on this form offer FREE shipping in the U.S.A</u> - Nevada residents add 7% tax - Mail this order to (S*hipping outside the U.S.A please inquire by mail.*)
Price good through 2005

_____
Name
_____
Address
_____
City   State   Zip   Phone

_____Check or Money order Enclosed (make check to **L.Buron**)

Signature_____

L. Buron
P.O. Box 12
Wellington, NV 89444

To:_____

Address:_____

City:_____

State:_____Zip_____

Mailing Label - Please Print Clearly

Include>Check, Order Form & mailing label